THE RECOVERY
OF THE
ANCIENT HEBREW
LANGUAGE

T0344386

THE RECOVERY
OF THE
ANCIENT HEBREW
LANGUAGE

AN INAUGURAL LECTURE DELIVERED
ON 30 JANUARY 1939

by

DAVID WINTON THOMAS
M.A.

Regius Professor of Hebrew in the
University of Cambridge

CAMBRIDGE
AT THE UNIVERSITY PRESS
1939

CAMBRIDGE
UNIVERSITY PRESS

University Printing House, Cambridge CB2 8BS, United Kingdom

Published in the United States of America by Cambridge University Press, New York

Cambridge University Press is part of the University of Cambridge.

It furthers the University's mission by disseminating knowledge in the pursuit of education, learning and research at the highest international levels of excellence.

www.cambridge.org
Information on this title: www.cambridge.org/9781107676428

© Cambridge University Press 1939

First published 1939
Re-issued 2014

A catalogue record for this publication is available from the British Library

ISBN 9781107676428 Paperback

THE RECOVERY
OF THE
ANCIENT HEBREW LANGUAGE

An inaugural lecture, as I understand it, should not aim in the first place at originality, but rather at presenting a more or less general account of some main problem connected with the lecturer's special field of study and the modern methods of investigating it. I propose, therefore, to speak on this occasion upon a problem which above all others is claiming the attention of Hebraists at the present time. This problem may be described as the recovery of the ancient Hebrew language. This subject is appropriate for this occasion, I venture to think, for another reason also. It is of importance not only for the Hebrew specialist, but also ultimately for all those who are concerned to see that the Old Testament is properly understood. For obviously, sound exegesis of the Old Testament must depend, first, upon the

〈 5 〉

establishment of the correct Hebrew text, and secondly, upon a right interpretation of it. And there can be no right interpretation of the Old Testament which is not based upon an exact knowledge of the Hebrew language. Among those present here there will be many who are not Hebraists, and it may appear that I have laid upon myself a difficult task in undertaking to speak upon a subject which falls within the sphere of the linguistic and textual study of the Old Testament. My hope is, however, that in spite of the technical nature of my subject, I may be able to convey to the inexpert something of the general problem; and I hope I may at the same time furnish the expert with an idea or two which may be found to be suggestive.

What then is the nature of our problem? Why must we speak in terms of the recovery of the ancient Hebrew language? Have we not the Old Testament, and is not that a sufficient basis for the study of Hebrew? To ask this question is at once to lay bare the problem. We have the Old Testament—but how meagre a monument it is of a people's literature! It is important, for the proper understanding of the problem before us, that clear recognition should at the outset be given to the fact that the Hebrew literature which the Old Testament preserves is but a part, and a small part, of an extensive Hebrew literature, which has otherwise failed to survive. How extensive a literature the Hebrews possessed we can only guess. We cannot, therefore, with any certainty measure our loss. But certain considerations point to the disappearance of a considerable Hebrew literature. We think, for example, of the lost books to which the Old Testament itself refers—the Book of Jashar (Josh. x. 13, 2 Sam. i. 18), the Book of the Wars of the Lord (Num. xxi. 14), and so on; of the loss of literature which must inevitably have resulted from the process of editing through which the Old Testament has passed—how much northern literature, for example, did the Judaean editors reject? And again we think of the fact that many, if not most, of the apocryphal books were originally written in Hebrew. Considerations of this kind impress upon us the essential fact that the Old Testament, representing as it does a very small part of the literature of the Hebrews, can preserve only a fraction of the Hebrew language. It cannot then of itself provide a sufficient basis for the study of ancient Hebrew. It should be remembered, in addition, that some parts of it have little or no value for the Hebraist—those parts, for example, which are merely genealogical or repetitive.

The inadequacy of the Old Testament as a basis for the study of ancient Hebrew is heightened if we consider some of those external influences which, we may suppose, affected the language, but of whose effect little or no trace now exists. Just as in our study of Old Testament history we are aware of gaps in our records, so in our study of the language are we aware of similar lacunae. If, for example, we may see in the Hebrew conquest of Canaan part of a larger Ḥabiru movement,[1] what elements may not that mixed horde of peoples have contributed to the later Hebrew language?[2] Other nomadic incursions into Palestine, whether in pre-historic or in historic times, will not have been without their effect too upon the language. Again, the language of the Old Testament betrays hardly any Philistine influence. But may we not wonder, as we read Old Testament history, whether that influence was not greater than our records suggest? And are the few Egyptian words in the Old Testament a true index of the influence of that language upon Hebrew? At certain periods, for example in the reign of Solomon, that influence may have been very great. What 'Phoenicianisms' too may not have been introduced during the Jezebel régime? And further, we think of the events of 721 B.C. and 586 B.C.—to say nothing of other invasions and deportations—with their disruptive influences not only upon the history and religion of Palestine, but also upon its language. Something of what took place after 721 B.C. we know from the Old Testament—how Samaria was peopled with Aramaic-speaking settlers from Mesopotamia (2 Kings xvii. 24), with the result that from this time onwards the north probably became bilingual; while after 586 B.C. came encroachments on the land by Edomite and other desert peoples from the south.[3]

The problem of the recovery of the ancient Hebrew language springs then from the fact that the Old Testament is a small volume of literature, which preserves only in part the full richness of the Hebrew language, and betrays but little of the many influences which must, in varying degrees, have left their mark upon it. It offers in consequence a very restricted field of enquiry for the study of ancient Hebrew. Certainly if we had to rely upon it alone we could scarcely hope to advance much further in our knowledge of the language. What means are then available whereby we may extend our knowledge of ancient Hebrew? First, and most important, we have the science of comparative Semitic philology. Here again we are conscious of a sense of loss. For some members of the Semitic group have vanished, some leaving a few traces, others none, behind them. Of the language of the Amorites, the Ammonites, the Amalekites, the Kenites and others we know little—in most cases, nothing at all. We can go little further than to suppose that they stood in a near relation to Hebrew. The Moabite Stone at least shows that the differences between Moabite and Hebrew were only dialectical.[4] The sudden appearance a few years ago of the 'Hebraic' dialect of Ras Shamra—of which I shall have more to say later—well illustrates how a Semitic tongue could fall into oblivion. Its recovery only emphasizes the loss of others. But against such losses may happily be set greater gains. Since the nineteenth century the science of comparative Semitic philology has been firmly established through the study of the greater Semitic languages—Accadian (i.e. Assyrian and Babylonian), Aramaic and Phoenician, Arabic and Ethiopic. As knowledge of these languages has increased, so Hebrew, which belongs to the same Semitic family as they do, has been gradually and remarkably illuminated.

The major problem in the recovery of ancient Hebrew is the development of Hebrew from proto-Semitic to the form in which we now find it in the Old Testament. By proto-Semitic is meant the assumed parent language which the Semites are supposed to have spoken in Arabia when they all lived together there before they migrated thence to people those parts of the Near East where later they are found. It is not possible, of course, to reconstruct proto-Semitic. Indeed there are difficulties in the very assumption of such a parent language with a common stock of words and a common grammar. The study of comparative Semitic philology, however, demonstrates that such a hypothesis is not only useful but necessary. This does not mean that we postulate a complete identification of vocabulary and grammar for all the Semitic languages in their earlier stages. There is obviously much in the several languages that cannot be fitted into any proto-Semitic scheme. But it does mean that the Semitic languages were less clearly defined in their earlier than in their later stages. I may here quote Professor G. R. Driver —'Early inscriptions', he writes, 'show Phoenician and Hebrew and Aramaic and even Arabic in a stage of development in which they stood in almost the same relation as Babylonian and Assyrian to each other and must indeed not so very far behind this stage have been a single language; it cannot therefore be considered surprising if idioms, present in regular use in this, are found sporadically also in that language, whether as isolated survivors from the common parent stock or as stray loans from the one to the other sister Semitic language.'[5] It is a fundamental position of the modern study of Hebrew that the Hebrews shared with their fellow Semites certain linguistic characteristics which now may be only or most clearly observable in the sister languages, and which, through the study of these languages, can be recovered for Hebrew. To-day we recognize that Hebrew was from the beginning a highly mixed language.[6] By the time we meet it in the Old Testament it has assimilated a variety of linguistic phenomena drawn from many sources. As the modern study of ethnology has revealed the mixed character of the ancestry of the Hebrews, so comparative Semitic philology has revealed the mixed character of the Hebrew language. By the gradual extrication of the diverse elements which have gone to compose it, its vocabulary is being enriched and its grammar explained. In the sphere of syntax too the same mixed character is evident. The Hebrew verbal system is now seen to be composed of elements characteristic of the eastern and western groups of the Semitic languages, Accadian and Aramaean elements predominating. In this sphere we may note the interesting and important recovery of two forgotten Hebrew tenses—a present-future and a preterite—in the light of which the difficulties surrounding the Hebrew construction with *waw* consecutive seem nearer solution than ever before.[7]

In the recovery of ancient Hebrew by means of the other Semitic languages Arabic plays an important part. At one time indeed, and it is not so very long ago, scholars depended almost entirely upon Arabic—with Aramaic—for their elucidation of Hebrew. The legitimacy of its use has, however, not always remained un-questioned. And still to-day there are some who accept it a little uneasily. No problem is involved, of course, in the use of Accadian for the elucidation of Hebrew, for Accadian litera-ture can boast an antiquity far greater than can Hebrew literature. There can be no question either of the validity of the use of Phoenician and Aramaic for this purpose, for documents in these languages survive from an early period. But Arabic comes late on the scene as a literary language—some eight hundred years or so later than the latest literature in the Old Testament. Is it not dangerous, therefore, even absurd, it is sometimes objected, to utilize this youthful language for the recovery of a language whose literature is centuries older? Dangerous it may be, but it is not absurd. The apparent absurdity disappears when once certain facts are fully comprehended. Attention may be drawn to three points especially. In the first place, we may reiterate the fundamental fact, familiar to every Semitic scholar, that Arabic, in spite of its youthful literature, is in many respects a far older language in a philological sense than Hebrew with its more ancient literature. It preserves, for example, many primitive grammatical forms which Hebrew has lost. It preserves, in fact, much that is far older even than Accadian. This statement must not be taken to imply that Arabic can lay any claim to exclusive priority above the other Semitic languages. For no Semitic language can such a claim be made. Yet there is truly a sense in which, as Dr S. A. Cook, my distinguished predecessor, writes, 'Arabic enables us to understand what is genuinely "Semitic" in the Semitic languages'.[8]

In the second place, there is the important fact that we are no longer dependent to-day for our knowledge of Arabic upon late sources. It can in fact be traced far back into the pre-Christian era. We have first the highly important inscriptions from South Arabia. Through them the history of pre-Islamic Arabia can be traced back to about 1000 B.C., perhaps even earlier.[9] If the inscriptions themselves do not extend as far back as this, they yet enable us to see what Arabic was like a thousand years and more before it became the language of the Qur'an. Only a few points in illustration of their significance for the study of Hebrew can be mentioned here. The fact that some common Hebrew words, which are scarcely known to classical Arabic, were already in use in Arabia at this early period cannot fail to impress us.[10] Significant is it too that sometimes a difficulty in the Old Testament can be explained only by reference to the vocabulary of the inscriptions.[11] Very valuable also is the light the inscriptions throw on Hebrew proper names. Not only are many of the well-known names of the Old Testament common in them, but, further, the current explanations of some of them can now be corrected by reference to the old Arabian language.[12] Secondly, under this head we may note that in north Semitic epigraphic records too we find means of tracing Arabic back to an early period. Professor Driver's statement, already quoted, will be recalled in this connection. What we may style 'Arabisms' are met with, for example, in the Aramaic inscriptions belonging to the eighth century B.C. from Zenjirli[13]—and earlier still in the fourteenth-century tablets from Ras Shamra.[14]

In the third place, inscriptions are not the only means we have of tracing Arabic back into the pre-Christian period. To-day the high value of the Septuagint in this respect is being gradually recognized. The Septuagint translators frequently translate the Hebrew text in such a way that their translations can only be explained on the assumption that they gave to a Hebrew word a meaning which to-day can only be recovered from Arabic. I touch on this point briefly here as I shall return to it again in a moment.

In richness of vocabulary classical Arabic leaves all the other Semitic languages behind. For the recovery of the ancient Hebrew vocabulary it provides an almost inexhaustible treasure-house. Its copious vocabulary is, of course, in part the result of later development, and care must therefore be exercised in the exploration and use of it. We need not, however, hesitate to regard it as axiomatic that the vocabulary of classical Arabic preserves much that is primitive. We meet here with a linguistic phenomenon which is constantly making its appearance in the study of comparative Semitic philology. I refer to the re-emergence in late literature of words which themselves are very ancient, and which may or may not be, through pure accident, attested in earlier documents. Hebrew itself offers many an interesting illustration of this. If, for example, we had only Ben Sira, should we not be tempted to argue that the word '*šwḥ* 'reservoir' (l. 3), not occurring elsewhere in Hebrew, is a late word? And yet it is to be found on the Moabite Stone (lines 9, 23)![15] Since the ninth century B.C. this old Semitic word lay hid until it turned up again seven hundred years later in Ben Sira. Mishnaic Hebrew too, it can be shown, preserves many a survival from an antique vocabulary. For example, the well-known word *ḥazzān* 'superintendent, officer' is the same word as *ḫazānu* 'prefect, regent', which occurs in the Tell el-Amarna letters.[16] Likewise in classical Arabic countless ancient words survive which, in spite of their antiquity, may happen to appear for the first time in the works of the classical Arabic writers. It is the recognition of this fact, combined with the fact that to-day we have means, as already shown, of tracking down some of the more ancient elements in the Arabic vocabulary, that justifies our use of the enormous vocabulary of classical Arabic for the recovery of the ancient Hebrew vocabulary.

The use of Syriac and Ethiopic for the elucidation of Hebrew also causes uneasiness in the minds of some, for their literatures too are late, being for the most part of Christian origin. This question need not detain us long, for what has been said about the use of Arabic applies in part also to the use of these two languages. It may be pointed out that both Syriac and Ethiopic can, like Arabic, be traced back through the Septuagint to the third century B.C. at least;[17] and that in both languages survivals of ancient Semitic usage are to be found. Of

Ethiopic in particular two additional remarks may be made. First, there are clear indications that in its earliest period of development it had a much closer affinity with Hebrew than appears in the later form of the language.[18] And secondly, common words which Ethiopic shares with Hebrew are not likely to have been borrowed by Ethiopic from Hebrew; rather were such words taken with them by the emigrants from their common home[19]—they are, in other words, proto-Semitic.

The legitimacy of the use of Arabic, Syriac and Ethiopic in our attempts to recover Hebrew is then beyond question. As was remarked above, we are not unmindful that this line of study has its dangers. A merely mechanical use of these languages may result in an explanation of Hebrew as arbitrary as any emendation of the Hebrew text. But the overwhelming evidence which comparative Semitic philology can produce completely vindicates this method of research. Hebrew, being a mixed language, shared with Arabic, Syriac and Ethiopic many of the characteristics and much of the vocabulary of these languages; and through the study of these sister languages we are able to recover for Hebrew ancient features of Semitic grammar and vocabulary which its own limited literature does not preserve. Nor too must the field of modern Palestinian and Syrian Arabic be neglected; for we may expect to find therein relics of the classical rules and ancient roots which, for one reason or another, did not pass into the classical language.[20]

How ancient Semitic words can be recovered through the Septuagint has already been pointed out. For the recovery of Hebrew it is by far the most important of the ancient Versions of the Old Testament. Whatever the merits or demerits of the Septuagint translators as Hebraists may have been—and that question will continue to be debated—they certainly retained a correct tradition as to the meanings of many Hebrew words, which are only to-day being recovered by means of the cognate languages. In the past it has been too readily assumed that where the Septuagint does not obviously represent the Hebrew text, the Greek translation reflects a different Hebrew text. To-day, however, many a Greek rendering, which at first sight appears not to reflect the Hebrew text, is seen, through Semitic research, to reflect the Massoretic, and not another Hebrew text. We must not suppose, however, that the Greek translators were in any sense Semitic scholars. In translating the Hebrew text they were not conscious of the fact that the meanings which they assigned to Hebrew words were shared by Hebrew with Accadian, Arabic and so on. They only knew that the Hebrew words in their day bore these meanings. Many of these traditional meanings, with which they were perfectly familiar, have since their time been lost. They can be recovered to-day for Hebrew only through the cognate roots in the sister languages. So do the Greek translators force upon us once again the conception of a common stock of Semitic words. Their translations, even though they may preserve a true tradition as to the meanings of Hebrew words, are, of course, not necessarily always correct. Yet even their mistranslations have a value, for from them lost Semitic roots may frequently be recovered.[21]

For the recovery of ancient Hebrew other languages, besides the Semitic, must be employed. The number of languages which the Hebraist to-day must take into account is growing alarmingly large. His horizon must include Sumerian, Egyptian, Persian and Greek. And even these do not exhaust the list, for there are other languages which, as the knowledge of them progresses, are seen to be of increasing importance for the study of Hebrew, for example, Hittite. And on the fringe of our study lie yet other tongues. One of the most remarkable discoveries of recent times has been the establishment of the Horites—hitherto regarded as a legendary pre-Edomite race, and, through false etymology, as cave-dwelling folk—as a real Mesopotamian people, the Hurrians,[22] who about 1900 B.C. moved westwards into Palestine and left their mark on Hebrew civilization, especially in the domain of law. From now on Hurrian must be reckoned among those languages which the Hebraist cannot ignore. The entry of the Horites upon the stage of history prompts the question whether some of those other peoples hitherto regarded as mythical— for example, the Rephaim or the Bene 'Anaqim —will at some future time turn out to be real peoples with a language and civilization of their own.

We have already touched briefly upon the contribution which Semitic epigraphy is making towards the recovery of Hebrew. Something may now be said of the contribution made by documents written in ancient Hebrew. Such documents are, as is well known, few in number. All the greater welcome, therefore, is accorded to the discovery of any additional material. And here mention must be made of a recent discovery which, with another soon to be named, will make the present decade a memorable one in the annals of Biblical archaeology. I refer to the discovery of the Lachish letters in 1935,[23] the most valuable find yet made in the Biblical archaeology of Palestine. Our Palestinian records are on the whole a disappointing source for the recovery of the ancient Hebrew vocabulary. They add surprisingly little in this respect. This is unfortunately true also of the Lachish ostraca. Though they provide some ninety lines of legible Hebrew, they scarcely add any new words. It is possible that when greater agreement has been reached regarding some of the readings other new words may be found to occur therein. But they will not be many. The importance of these ostraca lies elsewhere than in the sphere of lexicography. It lies in the certainty they afford that our Hebrew Bible is written in the genuine ancient Hebrew language. We know from them the kind of Hebrew the men of Judah were using in the age of Jeremiah, and a comparison between the language of the ostraca and the language of the Old Testament reveals their essential identity. It is for this, and for their further contribution to our meagre knowledge of Hebrew palaeography, that these letters from Lachish are of such high significance. The discovery of further ostraca of this kind is much to be hoped for. Continuous Hebrew texts such as these letters provide—and if we except the Siloam inscription, provide for the first time— have a value for the study of the Hebrew language which short and isolated fragments have not.

It is to Ras Shamra on the Syrian coast that we have to look for the second great archaeological discovery of recent times. The tablets unearthed there in 1929 and succeeding years are the most important epigraphic monuments ever found in Syria.[24] It will be possible here only to indicate in brief terms something of their significance for the study of Hebrew. There is as yet no agreement as to precisely what the language is in which they are written. For our present purpose we are content to style it, as we have done earlier, vaguely 'Hebraic'. These tablets, older than almost anything in the Old Testament, push the history of Hebrew back to the middle of the second millennium B.C. In view of what has been said earlier regarding the mixed character of Hebrew at an early stage, it is of great interest to note that this 'Hebraic' dialect of the Ras Shamra texts is also highly mixed, being composed of various Semitic and other elements. The value of these tablets for the study of early 'Arabisms' has been mentioned. It is indeed noteworthy how often the vocabulary of Ras Shamra is explicable from south rather than north Semitic.[25] It cannot be said that these tablets, like the Lachish ostraca, disappoint in the matter of the light they throw on the Hebrew vocabulary. On the contrary, they will, it is safe to forecast, effect something like

a revolution in Hebrew and Semitic lexicography. One interesting fact they reveal is that
words which in the Old Testament are ἅπαξ
λεγόμενα must have been in far more frequent
use than their isolated occurrence in the Old
Testament would suggest. An interesting example may be given. In Is. xxvii. 1 Leviathan
is described as a 'swift' and 'crooked serpent'.
The two epithets in Hebrew are respectively
bārīaḥ and ʿaqallāṭôn, the latter occurring no-
where else in the Old Testament. And yet here
it is on the Ras Shamra tablets in this same sense,
and what is more, it is used there, in conjunction
moreover with the word bārīaḥ, of a creature
called ltn, the primitive form perhaps of the
word Leviathan.[26] The twenty-seventh chapter
of Isaiah is generally regarded as part of a late
section of the book of Isaiah. We meet once
again, therefore, with an example of that phenomenon, referred to above, whereby a word is
lost sight of for centuries only to turn up again
at a later date. It is not only in the realm of
lexicography that these tablets are of such great
importance. The problem of the Hebrew tenses,
for example, will have to be studied in the light

of the Ras Shamra use of the tenses. There is much about the latter that is as yet obscure. But we note with the greatest interest the use at Ras Shamra of the *yqṭl* form as the narrative tense, for it links up with the proto-Semitic *yáqṭul* which underlies the preterite tense which we now recognize in the Hebrew *way-yiqṭōl*.[27]

We may turn now for a few moments to another aspect of our problem. It is the question of the pronunciation of ancient Hebrew and its relevance for the recovery of ancient Hebrew grammar. Until comparatively recently Hebrew grammarians have been content to recover the rules of Hebrew grammar on the basis of the vocalization which the Massoretes of Tiberias, with a view to the establishment of a correct pronunciation of Hebrew and correct recital of the Hebrew Bible in the synagogue, fixed once and for all about the eighth to the ninth centuries A.D. The application of their system of vocalization throughout the whole of the Hebrew Bible, to the earliest as well as to the latest documents, has had the effect of making it extremely difficult to trace the historical development of the language. If we would do this, we must endeavour to go behind the late, uniform system of the Massoretic vocalization and recover the pronunciation of Hebrew in earlier days. The recovery of this earlier pronunciation and the study of Hebrew grammar are intimately connected the one with the other. For the recovery of the earlier pronunciation brings with it the recovery too of ancient forms which at one time were a real part of the language, but which have been levelled out of existence through the schematic uniformity of the Tiberian system of vocalization. Can we know then how ancient Hebrew was pronounced? I must pass by with a bare mention the evidence for the pronunciation of Hebrew in the earlier period which is furnished by the Canaanite glosses in the Tell el-Amarna letters, by the Ras Shamra material, and by Egyptian and Accadian transliterations of Canaanite names. For the pre-Massoretic pronunciation of the Hebrew text itself we have to rely principally upon the transliterations which have been preserved, notably in the Septuagint, the Second Column of Origen's Hexapla, and in the writings of St Jerome.[28] The methodical use of these transliterations is, it must be confessed, far from easy.[29] The Greek and Latin alphabets, for example, have no exact equivalents of the Hebrew gutturals and sibilants;[30] and again proper names, which bulk large in this material, are notoriously liable to corruption. Yet, though their use calls for the exercise of great care, they do make it possible to go behind the Massoretic tradition and to recover evidence which points distinctly to a diversity of pronunciation at different periods in the days anterior to the Massoretes. They show us, to take a few simple examples, that the pronunciation of segholates during the period they cover was not uniform;[31] that the article was always pronounced with an 'a' vowel, even before a *ḥêth* with *qāmeṣ*;[32] that the doubling of the following consonant after the article is no older than the Second Column of the Hexapla;[33] and that St Jerome knew of no differentiation between the sounds *śin* and *šin*.[34]

The transliterations then make it abundantly clear that the Hebrew text could be read differently from the Tiberian text. In revealing an earlier stage of Hebrew pronunciation they reveal at the same time an earlier stage in the development of the Hebrew language. A like result emerges from the study of Hebrew Biblical manuscripts which are vocalized otherwise than according to the Tiberian system, especially those vocalized according to the Babylonian system of punctuation.[35] They too enable us to catch a glimpse of the vocalization of the Hebrew text at an earlier stage of development than that which is exhibited in the Tiberian text, and to recover ancient features of Hebrew grammar which are not, or which are only in part, recoverable from the Tiberian text. The evidence of the pre-Massoretic material compels us indeed to make a clear distinction between the grammar of ancient Hebrew and Tiberian grammar. The two are far from being always identical.

In this lecture an attempt has been made to show how the problem of the recovery of ancient Hebrew is forced upon us through the limited field of enquiry which the Old Testament offers, and how this recovery is being effected. We have seen something of the contribution towards this recovery that is being made by comparative

Semitic philology and the study of other languages, by the study of the Versions, especially of the Septuagint, by Semitic epigraphy, and by investigation into early Hebrew pronunciation. There are, of course, many other aspects of our problem on which we would, if time were available, willingly linger. There is, for example, the question of the recovery of Hebrew dialectical variations. The relative seclusion of some parts of Palestine and the frequent movements of peoples on Palestinian soil and the consequent intermixtures of populations permit us to take the growth of Hebrew dialects for granted. Yet it is no easy matter to distinguish them. Indeed, in the opinion of some, little certainty can be achieved in this matter. In certain parts of the Old Testament, however, notably in the Elohistic document and in the books of Judges, Kings and Hosea, clear traces of a northern dialect, strongly tinged with Aramaic, can be discerned.[36] Some interesting questions suggest themselves here. Can the characteristic features of the northern and southern dialects of Palestine be more exactly determined than at present? What contribution has Semitic epigraphy to make here? And may we look for help to the Samaritan Version of the Pentateuch, representing as it does a northern recension of the Torah, as the Massoretic text represents it in a Judaean recension?[37]

Passing reference may also be made to one other aspect of our problem. At the beginning of this lecture I remarked upon the importance for the sound exegesis of the Old Testament of the establishment of the correct Hebrew text. In view of the special value which attaches to the Septuagint in this connection, it is tempting to enlarge upon the significance of the Chester Beatty papyri, upon the early textual forms of the Greek Bible they afford,[38] and upon the discovery among them of a further copy of the original Septuagint Version of Daniel.[39] Or we might turn our minds to a consideration of the attempt by F. X. Wutz to recover the original Hebrew text on the supposition that the Septuagint translators had before them not a text in Hebrew characters, but a Greek transcription text.[40] But upon these, and upon other problems, no less fascinating, we cannot now dwell. For we have still to refer to three considerations which emerge clearly from the study of the problem before us.

The first concerns the field of Hebrew lexicography. The recovery of Hebrew has advanced to a stage where an up-to-date dictionary, in which will be collected together all the information that is now available from the multifarious sources for our knowledge of the language, has become a primary need. And here a plea may be entered—if it be not an ideal aim—for the inclusion within it of non-Massoretic as well as Massoretic forms. For, as has been pointed out, much genuinely ancient material has been recovered from non-Massoretic sources.

In the second place, the recovery of Hebrew is leading to a new conception of the problems of Hebrew grammar. We cannot be content, as were the older grammarians, to describe the Hebrew language. Our aim to-day must be different. It must be the tracing of the historical development of the language. The publication in 1922 of Bauer and Leander's *Historische Grammatik der Hebräischen Sprache*—to which Paul Kahle, an outstanding scholar in the field of Massoretic study, contributed—marked the beginning of a revolution in Hebrew grammatical study.[41] Already we are perceiving that Hebrew grammatical phenomena, which before seemed inexplicable, appear in a new light, and are recognizable as relics of an older stage of the language. We see how forms, which have been thought to be exceptional, themselves come under rules; and we observe again how some current explanations of grammatical problems are mere inventions on the part of Hebrew grammarians. There can be little doubt where the main problem of Hebrew grammatical research lies in the future. A hope may be expressed that there will not be lacking a succession of scholars, competent and properly equipped, to carry out the tasks that lie ahead in this difficult field of Hebrew study.

And finally, what effect, it may be asked, is the recovery of Hebrew having upon our attitude towards the value of the Hebrew text of the Old Testament? Its effect is very clear. We are moving in the direction of a more conservative frame of mind. The conditions under which the Old Testament has come down to us make the legitimacy of conjectural emendation undeniable. Such emendations, however, should not be treated with more respect than they deserve. They are after all only what their name implies—they are conjectures—and they should not be treated as if they were proven facts. We recall Hugo Gressmann's striking words—'Zehn Konjekturen, von denen keine überzeugt, sind wie zehn Nullen, die keine Eins geben'.[42] A conjecture may be right—in fact, some brilliant guesses, which have in the past been made, have been vindicated by later scholarship. But, on the other hand, it may be hopelessly wide of the mark. Old Testament scholarship has nothing to gain from conjectural emendation when it is undisciplined and uncontrolled. There is, and must be, a place for it, however, if it is regulated in accordance with recognized canons. The formulation of canons of emendation is a task beset with very great difficulties. Yet the time has come when that task should be attempted.[43] The legitimacy of disciplined emendation must then be allowed. But it cannot be too frequently insisted that the Hebrew text must, wherever possible, be explained, and not explained away. In innumerable instances where it has in the past been thought to be wrong, more recent study has shown it to be right. We are not blind to the fact that corrupt passages exist; it would be strange indeed if they did not. And the difficulties they present must be boldly faced. Some of them may be for ever beyond our power to restore. Yet it is the clear verdict of Hebrew research to-day that the reputation of the Massoretic text stands deservedly high, and that for the serious study of the Old Testament it must, in spite of its imperfections, constitute the proper starting-point. So does the linguist point the way for the exegete.

NOTES

1. See S. H. HOOKE in *Record and Revelation*, ed. H. Wheeler Robinson, 1938, p. 359.

2. Cp. H. BAUER and P. LEANDER, *Historische Grammatik der hebräischen Sprache*, 1922, pp. 19 ff.; further H. BAUER, *Zur Frage der Sprachmischung im Hebräischen*, 1924, pp. 16 ff.

3. Cp. W. O. E. OESTERLEY and T. H. ROBINSON, *A History of Israel*, vol. ii, 1932, pp. 55 f.

4. See G. A. COOKE, *North Semitic Inscriptions*, 1903, p. 5.

5. *Miscellanea Orientalia, dedicata Antonio Deimel annos lxx complenti* (*Analecta Orientalia* 12, Rome, 1935), p. 70.

6. See further the present writer's article 'The Language of the Old Testament' in *Record and Revelation*, pp. 374 ff.

7. See G. R. DRIVER, *Problems of the Hebrew Verbal System*, 1936, especially chs. ix and xiv.

8. *The 'Truth' of the Bible*, 1938, p. 156.

9. See D. S. MARGOLIOUTH, *The Relations between Arabs and Israelites prior to the Rise of Islam* (Schweich Lectures, 1921), p. 7.

⟨ 39 ⟩

10. *Ibid.* p. 8.

11. *Ibid.* p. 25, where '*āzab* in Neh. iii. 8 is explained as meaning 'restore'.

12. *Ibid.* pp. 13 ff.

13. See G. A. COOKE, *op. cit.* p. 185.

14. See n. 25 below.

15. Cp. S. R. DRIVER, *Notes on the Hebrew Text of the Books of Samuel*, 1913, p. xc; and G. A. COOKE, *op. cit.* p. 10.

16. See J. A. KNUDTZON, *Die El-Amarna-Tafeln*, 1907, p. 856; F. BÖHL, *Die Sprache der Amarnabriefe*, 1909, p. 9; and *Cambridge Ancient History*, vol. ii, p. 321.

17. See the present writer in *Record and Revelation*, p. 397, and references there.

18. A. DILLMANN, *Ethiopic Grammar*, 1907, p. 10.

19. D. S. MARGOLIOUTH, *op. cit.* p. 8.

20. Cp. I. EITAN, *A Contribution to Biblical Lexicography*, 1924, p. 18.

21. With this paragraph cp. G. R. DRIVER in *Journ. of Bibl. Lit.* lv, pt. ii (1936), pp. 101 ff.

22. See further E. A. SPEISER, *Mesopotamian Origins*, 1931, ch. 5, and the same writer's *Ethnic Movements in the Near East in the Second Millennium B.C.*, 1933.

23. See further the present writer's article in *Journ. of Theol. Studies*, xl (1939), pp. 1 ff.

24. A full Ras Shamra bibliography may be found in S. H. HOOKE, *The Origins of Early Semitic Ritual* (Schweich Lectures, 1935), pp. 69 ff.

25. For the affinities of the Ras Shamra dialect with Arabic and Ethiopic, cp. J. A. MONT-GOMERY, *Zeitschr. für d. alttestam. Wiss.* Bd. xii (1935), p. 208; and T. H. GASTER, *Religions*, No. 18 (Jan. 1937), p. 32.

26. See J. W. JACK, *The Ras Shamra Tablets*, 1935, pp. 45 f.

27. See G. R. DRIVER, *Problems of the Hebrew Verbal System*, pp. 85 ff.; for the use of the tenses at Ras Shamra see J. A. MONTGOMERY and Z. S. HARRIS, *The Ras Shamra Mythological Texts*, 1935, p. 25, and Z. S. HARRIS, *Ras Shamra; Canaanite Civilisation and Language* (Smithsonian Report for 1937), pp. 496 f.

28. See especially E. A. SPEISER, 'The Pronunciation of Hebrew according to the Transliterations in the Hexapla', in *Jew. Quart. Rev.* xvi (1926), pp. 343 ff., xxiii (1932–3), pp. 233 ff., xxiv (1933–4), pp. 9 ff.; and A. SPERBER, 'Hebrew based upon Greek and Latin Transliterations', in *Heb. Union Coll. Annual*, xii–xiii (1937–8), pp. 103 ff.

29. Cp. K. Levy, *Zur masoretische Grammatik*, 1936, pp. 9 f.

30. Cp. A. Sperber, *op. cit.* pp. 113 ff.

31. *Ibid.* pp. 181 f. Cp. C. F. Burney, *The Book of Judges*, 1920, pp. 167 f.

32. Cp. A. Sperber, *op. cit.* pp. 137, 193.

33. *Ibid. loc. cit.*

34. *Ibid.* p. 115.

35. Special mention may be made of the following writings of P. Kahle: *Der masoretische Text des A.T. nach der Überlieferung der babyl. Juden*, 1902; *Masoreten des Ostens*, 1913; and 'Die hebr. Bibelhandschriften aus Babylonien', in *Zeitschr. f. d. alttest. Wiss.* Bd. v (1928), pp. 113 ff.

36. Cp. C. F. Burney, *op. cit.* pp. 172 ff. and *Notes on the Hebrew Text of the Books of Kings*, 1903, by the same writer, pp. 208 f.; H. S. Nyberg, *Studien zum Hoseabuche*, 1935, pp. 12, 22, 35, etc.; and S. R. Driver, *Introd. to the Literature of the O.T.*, 9th ed., 1920, pp. 188, 448 ff.

37. Cp. A. Sperber, *op. cit.* pp. 151 ff.

38. See F. G. Kenyon, *Recent Developments in the Textual Criticism of the Greek Bible* (Schweich Lectures, 1932), pp. 97 f., 105 ff.

39. *Ibid.* pp. 112 f.

40. Cp. the present writer in *Record and Revelation*, p. 396, n. 2.

41. Cp. further P. LEANDER, 'Einige hebr. Lautgesetze chronologisch geordnet', in *Zeitschr. d. Deutsch. Morgenländ. Gesellschaft*, Bd. lxxiv (1920), pp. 61 ff. See also J. Hempel's short sketch, 'Zur alttestam. Grammatik', in *Zeitschr. f. d. alttestam. Wiss.* Bd. iv (1927), pp. 234 ff.

42. *Zeitschr. f. d. alttestam. Wiss.* Bd. i (1924), p. 19.

43. Cp. P. VOLZ, *ibid.* Bd. xiii (1936), pp. 100 ff.

www.ingramcontent.com/pod-product-compliance
Ingram Content Group UK Ltd.
Pitfield, Milton Keynes, MK11 3LW, UK
UKHW020448010325
455719UK00015B/486